CHURCH HURTS
Can Make You
Bitter or Better

You Choose!

by Joyce L. Carelock

Acknowledgements

This book is dedicated to my family whom I love and respect dearly; I give honor and respect to God, because without Him I can do nothing. God has given me the will and to do of his good pleasure and I could not have come this far without Him. Special thanks to my husband of 21 years, Pastor George W. Carelock (Grace and Mercy Cathedral) for your love, support and encouragement through the years. To my three miracle children: Jamel, Melia, and Brandon. My hopes are that my children will catch hold of my vision and allow God's plan to unfold in their individual lives. I love you all dearly and want the best for all three of you. Special thanks to my spiritual father, Pastor Clarence Welch, (Prayer Tower COGIC), St. Petersburg, FL, who has advised and prayed for me through the years. I acknowledge Uncle George and Aunt Joyce McMillian, for believing in me and always being available to encourage and support my endeavors. I thank God for two special leaders who taught me to never stand before God's people without the anointing, and the power of prayer and studying: Elder George Hearon and Evangelist Velma Hearon, you both played an intricate part in my spiritual foundation that began at Panzer Gospel Service, Germany.

Thanks to my mother Mary H. McLaurin; grandmothers Lucille Christian and Katie B. McMillian, you all encouraged and inspired me through the years to succeed. To the special mothers that poured into my life: Mother Fannie Williams; Mother Maxine Henry; Supervisor Mabel Gibbons; Mother Hawk, Mother Snow, Mother Monroe, Mother Skinner, Mother Boykins, Mother Henderson and Mother Marilyn Welch; and to three special mothers who has changed my life for eternity: the late Mother Banks, Mother Gray and Mother Beatrice Harris.

I acknowledge some of my former Pastors that deposited seeds of righteousness in me and saw my God given abilities as an asset to their ministries: Bishop Charles D Williams, Superintendent Canty, and Superintendent Snow; to my friends and love ones that have supported me through the years: Betty Simmons, Courtney Smith, Tonia Bailey, Kathy LeCounte, Charlette Bryant, Darlena Herring, Jeanette Maxwell, Darlene Welch, Faith Hayes, Andre Nikoi, Rosa Montgomery, Annie Hines, Ella Farmer, Annie Davis, Angela Carelock, Kenneth Harris, Gregory Roberts, Jerome and David McMillian, Peggy Malloy, Leroy McLaurin, Anthony Walker, Wallace Hull, and Pastor and First Lady Macklin.

Last but not lease, I want to thank two special friends, Betty Harris and Fitzroy Delacoudray, they were instrumental in pointing out my abilities and encouraged me to not delay in getting this book in the hands of many hurting people. Thank you both for allowing God to use you on April 2, 2008 to deposit a seed of purpose in me. This book is the beginning of many to come!

Table of Content

Introduction

I dedicate this book to those who have experienced hurt and pain both in and out of the church. You may have thought that life would be different because you gave your life to Christ. You may have envisioned crying fewer tears and experiencing less sorrow and worry. Every day was going to be sweeter than the day before, or so you thought. But now that you are saved, the hellhounds appear to be heavy on your trail, and these demons act as if they were on special assignment to take you out and make you quit. Don't you know that a quitter never wins and a winner never quits? We can look in the book of Revelation to see the end of our story, and as overcomers, we win.

Although you might not always feel like a winner, know that God made provision for you before the foundation of the world. Prior to reading this book, maybe you thought that you were dealing with issues and hurts that were restricted to you only. Could you imagine that other people out there can identify with your hurts and relate to what you are feeling?

One day, you will be able to use your individual testimony and experiences to help others get over their hurts.

Relationship Hurts

Candi, a middle-aged Christian woman, experienced a great deal of hurt from a past relationship. She can identify with hurts that come from many sources, such as relationships, family, work, church, sickness, and death. Her motto is, "Everything is going to be all right". She really believes that God is in control of her life and that eventually things will work out for her good. But over a period of time, Candi lost sight of God and started allowing her situation to push her further away from God.

In the fall of 1986, Candi realized that she was pouring strength and energy into a relationship that was going bad. She was stripped of her self-respect, independence, confidence, and even her peace.

She walked around many days like an empty shell, waiting for someone to tell her what to do. When she tried to think on her own, her independence would cause problems for her; therefore, she felt this reaction was God's will for her life. She prayed and cried herself to sleep many nights, yet the verbal and mental abuse got worse. Candi tried with all her heart to hold onto this broken relationship. What she did not realize was that her mental and emotional scars would linger much longer than any physical scars.

One morning, Candi awakened and saw life differently, and she decided that now was the time to make a change. Although she had been fed a lot of negativity, she decided to trust God and go out on her own. She could not live this way any longer. Her life was going downhill, and nothing in this relationship could justify the harsh treatment. Candi found an apartment in an undesirable neighborhood, the only place she could afford. This new place was going to be a place of peace and harmony, or so she thought.

The Attack

One night during the fall of 1987, Candi lay in bed around 2:00 AM. Awakening abruptly, she noticed that the moon was shining brightly on an object at the door, and suddenly she heard a noise as the bedroom door opened. As she looked up, she saw a strange man standing in the doorway with a knife. Oh, what fear gripped her heart, for she could not believe someone had broken into her home! Candi yelled out and asked, "What are you doing here?" The man shouted for money, and then yelled and said, "Take off your clothes!"

As Candi began to follow his instructions, she stood there in such fear and distress. The only thing she could do was pray, asking God for help! All of a sudden, she turned around in the dark room and started throwing the attacker back and forth. Candi refused to give up, and finally she had the advantage over him. He yelled, "Ma'am, please let me go." Candi knew at that moment that God had given her supernatural strength to overtake this man. Although she had great fear, God helped her in the midst of this crisis. The man finally broke away from her and ran out of the house. After the police and paramedics arrived, they told Candi that two other women who lived on her street had been raped and killed that same night. The information she received humbled her, and she realized that God had a plan for her life.

A few days later, Candi fell on her knees in the living room, asking God to give her peace of mind. While weeping she said, "I would rather live in a doghouse with peace than in a mansion without peace." As a result of her attack, she began to find her way back to God.

The Healing

Three months after her attack, Candi received orders for Germany. While preparing to go overseas, she found herself praying, "God, send me a man that will love me and the children that I hope to have someday." The funny thing was that God had already sent her someone special, but she could not recognize him because of all the hurt and pain she had experienced.

15

In 1988, Candi married a wonderful man named Bran, and the couple served their first assignment together in Stuttgart, Germany. This town was a place of new beginnings for both Bran and Candi, yet some more healing needed to take place in Candi. The Master geographically relocated Candi and her husband so that the healing could take place while the Master did a work in both of them.

Many of you reading this book have been through some difficult relationships, and you feel as if you cannot handle the challenge that comes with hurts. You have done as many of us do. For safety, you have run into a new relationship with all the baggage from the old one weighing you down.

While in Germany, Candi began to learn how to stay with God regardless of what came her way. The Lord allowed Candi to experience some powerful teachings that carried her through the tough times. She later realized that God had a plan and purpose for her life and that no devil in hell could abort that plan. She settled in the fact that she was chosen and that God had allowed her head to be lifted and had taken away her reproach.

Candi's experience of the man breaking into her house was a testimony that she needed to share with others. That testimony brought deliverance to many throughout the years. She learned to have godly relationships and to trust God no matter what happened.

One night during Bible study while she was serving in Germany, an evangelist taught on the topic of forgiveness.

Candi was moved with overwhelming conviction because of the hatred she felt for her attacker. That night, she asked God to save the man who had attacked her and to help her forgive him. When she finished speaking to God, Candi felt such compassion for the offender that she was completely delivered and set free that very night from the chains of fear and unforgiveness that had held her hostage. God begin to teach her how to love and have compassion on her enemies and how to forgive regardless of the offense. Candi realized that this quality of compassion had moved Jesus to lay down His life for us all. After this divine enlightenment, Candi began to grow spiritually by leaps and bounds, and she realized that God wanted her to teach the gospel of Jesus Christ. God later called her into the ministry, and she served as a deaconess in Stuttgart, Germany.

Life was good for Candi and Bran. Everything seemed to be falling in place, then she found out she was pregnant. But two months later, she miscarried, and the news crushed her heart and Bran's. The nurse explained that the blood types Candi and Bran had were cancelling each other out and that Candi would not be able to carry a child full term. This news was not good, especially for a twenty-eight-year-old woman who felt that she was ready to settle down and have children. She could not imagine not being able to have children of her own. The news devastated Candi, and she consulted God about it. She did not tell many people what the nurse said, but she repeated what God said and what she believed: that

He would give her a boy child, because He is the giver of life.

After coming home from the hospital, Candi fell to her knees and wept while she turned her Bible to 1 Samuel 1. While weeping, she asked God to give her a male child, and she stated, "You said that You have no respect of persons. You did this miracle for Hannah, and I want You to do it for me." She rose from her knees and went to sleep.

When she awakened, an inexplicable peace came over her, and she was able to deal with this unfortunate situation. Candi and Bran accepted what God allowed and went on with their lives. Three months later, Candi conceived again, and she delivered a 6 lb 2 oz baby boy on March 1, 1990. This day was one of the happiest days of her life. One day after she came home from the hospital, she was walking through the house when she heard a voice say, "And I don't." She stopped, and immediately her mind went back to the prayer in which she had told God that He said He did not have a respect of persons. Oh, how happy she was to know that God had answered her prayers and that He took the time to answer her after her blessing was manifested!

God gave her joy and laughter again, and with His mercy, He gave her a testimony which confirms that God is the giver of life. No one can make her doubt His miraculous power. God proved to Candi that He has no respect of persons and that He is able to do exceedingly and abundantly above all that we ask or think (Ephesians 3:20).

As Candi and her family traveled for the military, she encountered many experiences and hurts in life. She spent countless days weeping and trying to overcome deep hurts, like the betrayal of friends and loved ones. Some of the experiences comprised sickness, hurt, rejection, isolation, and despair. God was employing Candi and her family for a particular mission each time they moved. But Candi found herself trying to hold onto seasonal relationships that would only hinder her purpose on her road to destiny. Some of her relationships were fruitful and meaningful, and they brought her considerable strength.

Church Hurts

Many of you think that, because you are walking in the newness of life, everyone else is traveling the same road. The mind you now have is the mind of Christ, and your sole purpose is to please God. You do not expect to deal with drama in the church. Everyone is on the way to heaven, and we are all so glad about our destination, as you think. You expect to see a noticeable difference between the unsaved and those who profess salvation (church folks). Do people who profess Christ purposely hurt others and plan their demise?

I don't think that saints, baptized, born-again believers do such things. The Bible declares, "By this shall all men know that ye are my disciples, if ye have love one to another" (John 13:35). If love does not mark an action, then that act is not of God. Jesus was the epitome of love, and therefore we know that, where we find no love, God is not there.

Church folks expect you to overlook their foolish acts of aggression, as if you were not human, but what is comical is

that God expects us to forgive these aggressors and move on.
"Vengeance belongeth unto me, I will recompense, saith the
Lord" (Hebrews 10:30); so let Him handle what happens to
those who cause misery.

Thank God for the Holy Spirit who discerns the very
intent of man's heart. But God forbid that we continue in sin
after we get saved. The Bible declares, "A brother offended
is harder to be won than a strong city: and their conten-
tions are like the bars of a castle" (Proverbs 18:19). And the
Bible also says, "With lovingkindness have I drawn thee"
(Jeremiah 31:3). No matter what our personal feelings are
towards others, we cannot allow the devil to use us as a tool
to dishonor God.

Your Position Can Hurt You

On two different occasions, God gave Moses instructions concerning the rock. In the first instance, Moses was
instructed to take the elders with him and to strike the rock
with his rod. In the second instance, Moses was told to take
his rod and Aaron with him and to speak to the rock. Moses
did not follow God's commands directly, and Moses and
Aaron paid a heavy price for disobeying God. To us, this
disobedience seems minute, but to God, "To obey is better
than sacrifice" (1 Samuel 15:22). Let's see what the Scripture
say about the heavy price Moses and Aaron paid.

And the LORD spake unto Moses that selfsame day, saying, Get thee up into this mountain Abarim, unto mount Nebo, which is in the land of Moab, that is over against Jericho; and behold the land of Canaan, which I give unto the children of Israel for a possession: and die in the mount whither thou goest up, and be gathered unto thy people; as Aaron thy brother died in mount Hor, and was gathered unto his people: because ye trespassed against me among the children of Israel at the waters of Meribah Kadesh, in the wilderness of Zin; because ye sanctified me not in the midst of the children of Israel. Yet thou shalt see the land before thee; but thou shalt not go thither unto the land which I give the children of Israel.

Deuteronomy 32:48-52

God knows what He is doing when He gives us instructions concerning His people. Moses was told to strike the rock once in the first instance, and he struck the rock once. In the second instance, he was told to speak to the rock, but in anger he struck the rock and called the people rebels. Believe me when I say that our wrong doings do not go unpunished. God checked Moses and let him know that Israel was His chosen people. The people belonged to God, not Moses. Oh, how God loves His people, even in our folly!

Maybe disobeying God was easy for Moses because he was allowed to stay in the position of leadership. As God kept him in place, he felt like many of us do, "Maybe I have gotten away with my sin, and maybe the sin of disobedience was not so bad. After all, God is still blessing." Does this reasoning sound familiar to you? How many of us know that we might get by other Christians, but we never get away from God? Moses did what many of us do. We continue as if nothing happened, but disobedience eventually catches up with us.

My bishop in Alaska once said that "God is the only man I know that will allow you to feel His presence and let you send yourself to hell". We are deceived many times by the presence of God; to think that He appeared because of someone's disobedient state is sad. Has the thought ever occurred to anyone that God will show up for one righteous believer, but His presence does not mean that you are the righteous one?

God rejected Saul also because of his disobedience. Saul was another example of one who was determined to do things his way and not follow God's instructions. As a result, God took His spirit from Saul and gave him an evil spirit. Every time David played the harp, the evil spirit would go away, but it would always come back once David stopped playing. The Spirit of the Lord had departed from Saul. Although he still retained his position of authority, he could not recognize that God had rejected him. Saul, like many today, stood under someone else's umbrella of anointing.

Encouragement to Move Forward

Please don't get stuck because of the hurt you receive in the church. "Wait on the LORD: be of good courage, and he shall strengthen thine heart: wait, I say, on the LORD" (Psalm 27:14). God is in control. He will not always move people who have wronged you, but be assured that they have not gotten away with their sin. Many of you have been in church with known fornicators, adulterers, liars, cheaters, and those who say that God said something that He did not say. Rest assured that our works will follow us into judgment. I admonish you to "gird up the loins of your mind" (1 Peter 1:13) and know that "all things work together for good to them that love God, to them who are the called according to his purpose" (Romans 8:28). Make sure to keep your heart pure, and do not allow the devil to use you to hurt others. "Bless them that curse you, and pray for them which despitefully use you" (Luke 6:28).

Let the hurt stop with you! Don't allow the devil to use you to reciprocate hurt and pain to others. Regardless of the amount of pain you have experienced, learn to be an advocate and to help others get relief. Stop sitting around feeling sorry for yourself because of what you have suffered. Use those hurts as an opportunity to move to higher ground in God.

Sometimes you might feel like no one knows or understand what you are experiencing. For me, my hurts seemed greater than anyone else's hurts because they were happening to me. You know how we are. Nobody is hurting or enduring hardship but us, or so we think. Trust me when I say that some people are hurting far more than you can imagine. My trials literally felt like they were going to take me out.

Recovery Time

Life would be so sweet if we could have recovery time between the hurts we encounter, before another bump or knock comes our way. But sometimes the hurts keep piling up, becoming mountainous to bear. Even if you are a strong person who does not complain, hurts can hit so hard that they can force you to step back and regroup. We find ourselves questioning our very foundations in the midst of the pain. In times like these, seeking the Master for His will concerning the situation is important. Learn how to stand still until His way is clear, because the situation could become worse if you move too quickly.

Forgiveness

Learn to forgive the transgressor even if he never asks for forgiveness. Stop sitting around waiting for someone to apologize for hurting you. If the apology does not come, then rejoice because you have peace with God. Stop allowing your hurts to hold your mind and heart hostage with bitterness.

Break loose everything that has come to bind your mind. Hurts have similarities. Look at some hurts you encountered before salvation and hurts you have encountered since salvation; pain is common to both.

Difficulty might come while trying to shake the hurt and pain you have experienced during your Christian journey. But hold your head high, for help is on the way. My advice to you is to deal with your issues and stop letting weights and sin linger in your individual life. Let these encumbrances go! Stop accommodating that furniture of hurt and pain in your spiritual house. The dead things in our lives must be purged away so that we can yield forth fruit that is fit for the Master's use. We should focus on doing the will of our Father and allowing God to have His way in us. Peter said about Jesus in the Word: "Casting all your care upon him; for he careth for you" (1 Peter 5:7).

Many times, people appear to have become professionals at getting hurt. Stop faking invulnerability! No matter how many times someone hurts you; every new assault reopens the wound and makes it more sensitive. A spiritual wound is just like a natural wound in this way: when you hit or scrape the wound, the pain becomes greater, because the sensitive area has been irritated.

Ladies, please deal with your pain, and stop taking it out on those around you. Take off the mask, and let God the Father heal you. Stop running around singing the "I Am Okay" song. That song will not heal you! The blood of Jesus is the only remedy for pain and hurt. As Christians, we must take literally everything to the Lord in prayer. God has given women endurance, and we normally can take a great deal of discomfort before we sink. A woman knows how to live with things that are uncomfortable or have caused her to become emotionally deformed. She might be hurting, but she learns how to keep on going as long as she has breath, because she thinks that persisting unfazed is the proper thing to do. Huh!

Many times, the hurt in our hearts comes out in our actions. Women are good at being cordial and fitting in, while looking as if everything is all right. Sometimes, people spend a lot more time looking good than they spend being good. Especially when the hurts come frequently and they do not want to give up, they learn how to bury those hurts on the inside and keep on moving. Putting on make-up just right, they think that no one can see through to the pain and hurt. They love a crowd because the attention is not on them and they blend in easily with others.

What happens when no one at home encourages you or understands what you are feeling? How do you pick yourself up from devastating situations that caused you to second-guess God? I know I have wondered: *What is it God? Did I sin, or have I done something to offend You? Please tell me, God; why are things working against me instead of for me?* I have literally had to lay hands on myself and intercede for myself and say, "Lord it is me; I am standing in the need of prayer." I did not understand why my hurts were continual, because I am one who will give my last strength for others. Sometimes I thought that maybe I wore an invisible sign that said, "Hurt Me"!

I admonish you all to "stand fast therefore in the liberty wherewith Christ hath made us free, and be not entangled again with the yoke of bondage" (Galatians 5:1). No more will you allow people to hurt you and leave you in an emotional rut; learn how to release your pain and move on. You are not a deep freezer; therefore, your job is not to store the hurt. You are a royal child bought by the power of God. Take the time to talk about what you are suffering, and seek after wise counsel. Do not go to someone who wants to know everyone's business, for those people themselves need a great deliverance. Ask the Father to direct you as to who to approach about your situation and when. Timing is everything, and sometimes when we move out of season, we do not understand why everything went wrong. Wait on the Lord!

The Church

Many people attend church, but the church is not in them. I visualize the church in a two-part view: the church triumphant and the church militant. The church militant comprises all kinds of people from different walks of life. The church triumphant comprises those blood-washed and baptized believers who understand their purpose in the body of Christ.

In the parable of the wheat and the tares, when the servants ask their master whether to uproot the tares that don't belong in the field, the master answers: "Nay; lest while ye gather up the tares, ye root up also the wheat with them. Let both grow together until the harvest: and in the time of harvest I will say to the reapers, Gather ye together first the tares, and bind them in bundles to burn them: but gather the wheat into my barn" (Matthew 13:29-30).

Many of us thought we were walking out of darkness into a glamorous new world with new people. Have you noticed that people who give their heart to Jesus are still human and still have issues like you do? We experienced hurt in the world, and guess what? We are still experiencing hurt in the house of God. Someone coined this phrase: "hurt people hurt people." This maxim is true; if an individual who has been hurt before does not get delivered, he will reciprocate what he has experienced. This saying is especially true for leaders and those who are in a position of authority. Being in authority can cause a major shipwreck for the gospel if the person is not delivered. That person has a voice that they can use either to bless or to curse the people. One would hope that, by now, saints would have a handle on their spirits and know when the enemy is at work. Paul admonishes us to die daily and to "be ye transformed by the renewing of your mind" (Romans 12:2).

The dreadful cycle of hurt has damaged, wounded, and killed many people in the church. No matter how hard you try to camouflage the pain inside, it is not hidden. You can cover bruises, scars, and cuts, but hurt to the heart shows in various forms that are noticeable. Some signs to recognize in people who have been hurt are: insecurity, anger, unforgiveness, jealousy, arrogance, self-centeredness, etc.

Even if the victim is you, you must get delivered and learn how to deal with the hurts. Hurt can interfere with your ability to trust and feel comfortable around others who really love you. You cannot always think that someone is out to hurt you, based on your past experiences. You must not stereotype everyone who tries to get close to you or to know you just because you think that the person has devised a plan against you.

Some of the hurts that I experienced from people in the church were difficult to bear. My expectation of how a Christian is supposed to act was biblically based; therefore, seeing other kinds of behavior than what the Bible prescribed threw me for a loop. I expected better from those who claim salvation and the presence of the Holy Spirit. Being hurt by someone you love and respect takes a lot out of you. I often thought: *Had this hurt come from my enemy, I could have borne it with ease, because I expect my enemy to lie to me and try to cheat me and steal from me.* But such assaults from my co-laborers in the gospel caught me off guard. Jealousy and unforgiveness are the responses of unbelievers, because they do not know any better; the gods of this world have blinded their minds. But to encounter this type of behavior in the house of God can dishearten and damage a lot of people.

I can remember going to church burdened with tears in my eyes and a wounded spirit, watching the persons whom the devil had used to hurt me shout all over the church. They appeared to be so free and full of the Spirit, while I was sitting silent, hurting. I guess this paradox is what the Bible means when it says, "having a form of godliness, but denying the power thereof" (2 Timothy 3:5); Paul is describing those who refuse to let God come in and clean them up from ungodly ways and habits.

I Was Bitter

I must confess that some hurts have caused me to be bitter in the past. Now that I am older and wiser, I know that this too shall pass, and I cannot afford to be bitter. Many days, I encouraged myself in the Lord. I never gave up on God, no matter what came my way. I put my trust in Him, because He is "the author and finisher of [my] faith" (Hebrews 12:2). My "life is hid with Christ in God" (Colossians 3:3); therefore, "I will not fear what man shall do unto me" (Hebrews 13:6). Through the years, I learned to do all things "heartily, as to the Lord" (Colossians 3:23), because if you do anything for the sake of man's approval, you will be disappointed. Man is fickle, but God is sovereign.

When I stop letting the negative comments and looks of others intimidate me, God began to do something different in my spirit. The Scripture came alive to me that say: "Fear not them which kill the body, but are not able to kill the soul: but rather fear him which is able to destroy both soul and body in hell" (Matthew 10:28). I began to look at life from a different perspective. I must say that one of my greatest deliverances was from church folks. If I am going to get to heaven, I must take in stride some things that are not pleasant. My grandmother used to say, "It might not be good to you, but it is good for you." And a friend of mine who resides in Alaska always says, "People can only do to you what you allow them to do."

You have no control over what a person does, but to a degree, you have control over what you allow to affect you. "Thanks be unto God, which always causeth us to triumph in Christ" (2 Corinthians 2:14), even in the worst situations. God has a way of taking what the enemy meant for evil and using it for our good. "Our God is a consuming fire" (Hebrews 12:29), and he is able to deliver us out of the snares of the enemy and put our feet on a rock to stay. I must say that, despite all the hurts I have received and the trials I have endured in life, I still have my joy, peace, and love.

Many of you are hoping for someone to love you for you, someone who does not have a hidden agenda. You know what you have suffered in life, and many times you have gone through periods of difficulty that made you feel like you have been to hell and back. The hurt and pain have caused you to be cold and callous, and you struggle with loving people. Your heart desires a person with whom you can share your precious secrets. You are tired of the games that people play, and you would rather be left alone than to be hurt again. You are in your own little shell, where you find yourself frequently in isolation. Deep inside, you long to share with someone what you have never felt: security and unconditional love. The person you are hoping to find one day appears to be a fantasy, and so you continue to keep on hold the thoughts and feelings that reside in your innermost being. Trusting people is hard for you because of your past rejections and hurts; therefore, you keep your guard up to protect your heart. Many times, you have failed in life because you were living up to the expectations of others.

Based on past hurts, the fear of moving towards the passion God has put in you causes you to doubt your abilities. Please learn how to express yourself, and be free from the pain inside. Let me reacquaint you with a perfect Friend and Confidant; His name is Jesus. He recognizes what you suffer, understands your hurts, and knows how to wipe every tear away. This Friend is real, and when you let your guard down to trust Him, He will lead you all the way. He specializes in loving you to the point of healing you. No matter what you have experienced, the Father knows how to draw you to Him with love and kindness. Many have lost sight of this Friend, while others have never known Him, but I can say with conviction that no other friend is like Jesus. I recommend Jesus for all of your difficulties right now, and I guarantee that He won't fail you.

Understanding your Attachments

Oh, how pleasant life would be if we only knew why God allows certain trials to come our way! I am confident that God knows what He is doing and that He will put no more on us than we are able to bear. "It is God which worketh in you both to will and to do of his good pleasure" (Philippians 2:13).

Most of our relationships in the church bring emotional attachments, especially if we allow ourselves to fellowship with the people of God. Make no mistake about it; these emotional attachments can interfere with the will and plan of God. We must go through various trials in order to reach the pinnacles that God has already set in place on our road to destiny. Just as God told Jeremiah, "Before I formed thee in the belly I knew thee; and before thou camest forth out of the womb I sanctified thee, and I ordained thee a prophet unto the nations" (Jeremiah 1:5). Oh, what consolation we have in knowing that God had a plan for us before the foundation of the world, before our fathers thought about getting with our mothers! Many times, Christians hold on to things and places from which God is trying to break them loose. Anything that hinders us can block us from our destiny.

Just like Lot's wife, we must leave the doomed city without looking back. Do not allow your heart to get attached to things that are temporal. If only Lot's wife could have understood that God needed her out of the city in order to destroy the people and the city! She did not see the provision that God was making for her. Lot's wife did what many of us do; she held on to what was familiar. Abraham prayed that Lot and his family be spared, but the emotional attachment of Lot's wife caused her destiny to be aborted. When you are forced to leave a place of comfort, take with you your emotions and your ability to stand. Do not let the enemy feed you a word of doubt or insecurity. God has a purpose and a plan for His people. Your destiny might be different from mine, but we must all know that God has destined us for greatness. Everything we are experiencing now is just the beginning of where He is taking us. The Master is calling us to a higher place in Him, and we must go!

Suicidal Tendencies

Stop letting your hurts cause you to commit spiritual suicide, by going on a spiritual hunger strike. So what if your mind is not clear and you do not feel adequate based on your current dilemma? Do not stop eating "the sincere milk of the word" (1 Peter 2:2). Do not allow fellowship to cease, and do not complain about everything. If your prayer bank is depleted and you have not fasted in months, you are spiritually hungry. I call all of these behaviors suicidal tendencies because they are detrimental to a Christian's spiritual health. Get yourself together, and declare that "I shall not die, but live, and declare the works of the LORD" (Psalm 118:17).

Regarding the children of God, the devil would like nothing better than "to steal, and to kill, and to destroy" (John 10:10). During the times of hurt and despair, we must take an inventory to see what we need in our individual lives and what we need to throw away. We might have to get rid of some folks around us who mean us no good. Fickle and negative, they always have a word of discouragement for us. Try spring-cleaning your spiritual house, and figure out what you have and what you need to eliminate. Do not focus on the storm but on where the Master is trying to take you. Peter is a witness: as long as he kept his eyes on Jesus, he did not sink and was able to walk on the water. I equate this story to the ability to stay afloat in the midst of danger and adverse circumstances. The moment Peter took his eyes off Jesus, he began to sink. No matter what we encounter as saints, our eyes must be fixed on Jesus.

Don't Give Up

Earlier in the 1980's, I encountered verbal and mental abuse that had handicapped my emotions, my self-esteem, and my love for God. These attacks taught me what happens when we give mere men too much control of our individual lives. During this time, I gave my life to God, and I experienced a mighty move that caused me to seek after more of God. I could read the Bible, and without trying, I could remember the Scriptures, chapter and verse. But the more I ran towards God, the harder life became, and the more issues I had to face.

God had anointed me mightily so that I could see in the spiritual realm. I would walk down the hall at work, pass a coworker, and see the spirit of the person, not his physical face. I saw heads that were like animals and various other things. This experience frightened me, because I did not have anyone at the time to help me understand spiritual gifts. At work once I met a lady whom I never seen before. When she was walking out of the door, I heard the Holy Spirit say, "Spirit of adultery," and I told the lady what God had said. This lady began to weep, and she repented right in the office, rededicating her life to God.

God would speak to me in an audible voice, only a word or two as I walked by the way. One morning as I was going to noonday prayer, I heard the voice of God say that He was El Shaddai. He spoke these words to me during a time when

I needed some encouragement just to live and did not know how I was going to endure. God took the time to let me know that He was more than enough. I had gone through the Bible several times, and I actually taught people from Genesis to Revelation during my personal time.

I was hurting, and because I did not know how to give my pain to God, I was on the verge of throwing in the towel. I felt the need for a tangible person who understood what I was suffering and was willing to give me wise counsel. But the more I inquired and sought for help, the more I was made to feel like a pilgrim in a foreign land. Without a clear understanding, all of this knowledge of God in the midst of my issues caused me to give up on my spiritual inheritance. I sold my birthright in exchange for hurt and pain. The exchange appeared to be fair at the time.

I felt like God was not concerned about what I was suffering. If He was concerned, why didn't He make all the hurt and pain go away? Many times, I sought after people whom I thought were spiritual and whom I could trust to give me a word of encouragement. I was sinking, and I did not know how to get my head above water. When I attempted to talk about what was happening to me, the devil was rebuked in me, and I was told to pray and give the hurt to God. My situations and challenges caused me to run away from God, and I ended up in a backslidden state. When trouble knocks at your door, you want answers, not someone telling you to pray. I was already praying, but I felt as if God was not answering quickly enough for me. I found myself drifting away from the teachings that I knew to be true. God was taking too long to vindicate me and to rescue me out of my troubles.

I helped myself by removing myself physically from the source of the hurt so that I could start over and take my life back. I was willing to sacrifice to get away from the pain and suffering that I was experiencing. In my backslidden state, the appetite for church as a whole died, and my desire was for worldly things. As I started to feed the lust of my flesh, I was getting further away from God and His plan for my life. When I encountered an opportunity to go back to church, I found myself sitting on the last row, crying through the sermon. What I was suffering had caused me to push God out of my life completely. But how many people know that God knows how to get you back on the road to your destiny?

From Test to Testimony

In the midst of everything happening in the church, I was having my own little personal battles. My health was not good, and I became sick a lot with head colds. In order to raise my son in a better environment, I decided to change my career while we were living in South Carolina. While adjusting to one income and learning how to be a domestic engineer, I found myself in another place that caused great distress. This period in my life was a time to settle down and know God for myself in the midst of my hurts.

My husband and I had an eighteen-month-old son, but our desire for another child appeared to be impossible. To me, God was the life-giver, and if He intervened for us once, surely He could do so again. While living in South Carolina, I miscarried three children, each around the fifth month. Each time, I had to undergo surgery. I learned how to give thanks in all things, for this pain was the will of God concerning me (1 Thessalonians 5:18). Giving thanks in difficulty is easier said than done, and I had to learn how to appreciate God in the midst of terrible grief in order to give thanks.

I did not understand why I had to go through those traumatic events. My life was completely sold out to God, and I sought His face daily. When the first child died, God comforted my heart and gave me peace. One day, I was driving home from the doctor's office while my husband was away in school, and I heard God speak clearly to me. He said, "Shall we receive good at the hand of God, and shall we not receive evil?" (Job 2:10). I immediately said, "Yes, Lord," and began to weep, because the Father took the time to ask me a question. This perspective from Him helped me to maintain my integrity and stay with God regardless of what was happening. The recovery from this first loss was quick, and I moved on with my life, doing the things of God in my everyday life.

The next loss happened about six months later. I found out I was pregnant, but this child died also. In the midst of this hurt, I wept and asked God what was happening. My relatives and friends told me that God was trying to tell me something and that I should just settle for the one son that I had. I could not receive any of their words, because I knew that God was the life-giver. In the midst of what I was suffering, God said to me, "Am not I better to thee than ten sons?" (1 Samuel 1:8). I wept and began to hold onto the son that I had, yet I still believed that God was the life-giver.

During my test of faith, a married woman I knew found out that she was pregnant and wanted to have an abortion. While lying in my bed at home the day before my final surgery, I talked her out of aborting her child. I never told her that I was lying home with a dead child in me. I encouraged her and even pledged to help her any way I could. The woman decided to keep her child, who is now fifteen years old and doing well. I thought that I was surely losing it, because in the midst of my hurt, I was helping others get free. I testified in church that I had learned to be content in whatsoever state I find myself (Philippians 4:11). I was at the breaking point, waiting on God to show Himself strong and mighty in this situation. I was ridiculed and ostracized, but I held fast to the testimony that God gives life and that I would eventually have another child one day.

Paul said, "That I may know him, and the power of his resurrection, and the fellowship of his sufferings, being made conformable unto his death" (Philippians 3:10). When trouble comes to our door, we sometimes forget all those Scriptures that we quote and hide in our hearts that we might not sin against God (Psalm 119:11). Many people could not have stood this test, because the hurt was so painful. In fact, no one else seemed to understand what mental anguish I was suffering.

When I became pregnant about seven months later, I felt that surely this child would live, because I responded to the last two deaths in the right spirit. I handled everything the Christian way. I did not ask God many questions; I thanked and praised Him for what He had done. When people had come to my house the last time to offer their condolences, I encouraged them. Surely this baby would live, because I had done everything according to how Christians should respond to hurt, or so I thought. I was confident that God felt that I had been through enough pain and that He was going to vindicate me with this child. I worked hard to make sure that I gave God thanks and praise every day for the great things He was doing for me. The baby was kicking and moving in my stomach, and God was being glorified in my body.

Well, that child died also. I remember going to the hospital hurt and unable to speak because I was so terribly disappointed. I only wanted to know what I was doing wrong. In my mind, I wondered if people were right in what they were saying about God trying to tell me something. Was God against me for some sin of which I was not aware? My mind was racing, trying to figure out what I could do or say to justify this baby dying. In the midst of this crippling agony, God was not speaking to me. It is one thing to suffer, but it is another thing not to hear from God in the midst of that suffering. I felt like I was in a dry and desolate place with no hope and no God on my side.

Nothing seemed to be helping me right then, and I had to screen my calls from all the negativity. This last death gripped my heart and shook my faith a little. I thought: *Where is Christ? What have I done to You, God, that You would allow me to suffer repeatedly? Yet You send people my way for me to help. I am not a monster. I have feelings, and I am hurting.* Even during this time, I was babysitting children that needed emergency help, yet my children were dying.

I went to the hospital for surgery, and I sat in a wheelchair while the nurses pushed me towards a back office to fill out some paperwork before surgery. My four-year-old son Chad was standing beside me at the time, holding onto the wheelchair. As the tears ran down my face, he looked up and yelled at his dad, saying, "Tell me, Dad; who is going to wipe my mama's tears? Tell me who?" The moment when he spoke, I broke down and cried like someone having a breakdown. The nurses all cried, and my husband began to pull my son out of the room. Chad pulled away from my husband, reached back for me, looked at the nurses, and said again, "Who is going to wipe my mama's tears; tell me who?"

That day, I understood what God was saying when He spoke a word to me after my second loss, saying, "Am not I better to thee than ten sons?" The son I had was better than ten sons. As I went home from surgery, I found myself clinging to that son and thanking God for allowing me to have a son that really loved me. On the inside, though, I had a strong desire to have another child, and I was still confident that God gives life.

That place of loss is still a mystery to me, but God the bishop of my soul knows all about it. He has a way of vindicating us in the midst of the storm, and I gave everything to Him. I thank God that I know Him for myself and that salvation is of the Lord, not of man. No one can make me doubt God. My life is hid in Christ (Colossians 3:3), and the life I now live is by the son of God that loved me and gave Himself for me (Galatians 2:20).

My Will vs. God's Will

God has a plan and a purpose both for His entire creation and for each individual. God does whatever He pleases, and He desires that all of us do His will. We must be mature in order to do God's will completely. God's will is always good, acceptable, and perfect (Romans 12:2). Jesus was our perfect example, because He was sustained for life.

The will of God leads to suffering sometimes. As Christians, we strive to know the will of God for our individual lives. We must be able to discern God's will through prayer and pray His will for the world. Jesus considered those who did God's will to be family members. Some of the greatest qualities in people develop through suffering, and therefore, is not suffering the will of God?

If we could be like Jesus and endure, we could grow. Christ the human was always completely yielded to His Father's divine will. Jesus naturally responded to God in perfect obedience. Paul tells us that the will of God leads to suffering. "For I reckon that the sufferings of this present time are not worthy to be compared with the glory which shall be revealed in us" (Romans 8:18). If the suffering we presently endure brings great hardship, cruel and unusual punishment, severe persecution, or even death itself, none of these evils can compare with the heavenly blessing that awaits those who are in Christ Jesus.

From Distress to Victory

After this season of great loss, my husband's job sent us to Alaska. This move came at a good time, because all of us in our family needed the change. Prior to leaving South Carolina, my husband had testified at Canty Memorial Church that God said I would have a baby by December of the upcoming year. The Lord also told my husband that what he bound on earth, God would bind in heaven, and what he loosed on earth, God would loose in heaven. My husband began to loose life in my body, binding the spirit of death.

After being in Alaska about six months, I realized that I was pregnant again, and the devil put in my mind not to acknowledge this child, because I already knew what was going to happen. As I was in my son's room, I heard clearly the Spirit of the Lord say, "Faith without works is dead" (James 2:26). Immediately, I grabbed my Bible and began to read those Scriptures, and I started to realize that I must walk in faith and that my works were the evidence that God would allow this child to live.

The next day, I went to the store and started buying baby items in order to prepare the nursery. Our family had joined a church in Alaska, where I was asked to speak, and at the end of my message, I made a faith statement. I stated that I was pregnant and that I was at the place in my pregnancy where the child normally dies, which was the end of the fifth month. I declared that this child would live and that this child would be very healthy! Many people marked my mouth that day and watched me carry my son. On March 1, 1995, I had a healthy baby boy, Denzel; his health report said that he was very healthy. All I can say is that God gives life without any intervention from the doctors.

I am so glad that trouble doesn't last always: "Weeping may endure for a night, but joy cometh in the morning" (Psalm 30:5). In the midst of everything that our family suffered, God vindicated me, and when I had my son, all the pain and suffering that we endured was over. The Master dried all my tears and blessed the fruit of my womb. In Alaska, my husband and I learned how to work and stay faithful to God no matter what happened. I feel that God had equipped me to be a confidant to many saints that needed someone to listen to them and pray with them.

I remember being attacked by my fellow sisters in the Lord over a position in which God had placed me. I kept on working and gave the attack to the Lord, and as I looked to Him, He fixed them and me. I stood fast and let the Lord fight the battle; I realized that I was no match for the devil or jealousy. Many times, such character sabotage and outright lies hurt my feelings, but I kept on working as unto the Lord (Colossians 3:23). Because I had a desire to live for God, He kept blessing and anointing me. No matter how anyone felt about me, no one could deny the anointing that God had placed on my life. God turned many relationships around through my faithfulness and love toward Him. With a conviction in my spirit, I stood on the Scripture: "Giving no offence in any thing, that the ministry be not blamed" (2 Corinthians 6:3). I had to "endure hardness, as a good soldier of Jesus Christ" (2 Timothy 2:3).

I can tell you about church hurt. I was at the altar one Sunday night while the altar call was going forth. The entire missionary board was gathered to help the souls at the altar. One missionary standing near me gave me a few choice words and rolled her eyes at me while at the altar. I looked at her with a smile and said, "God bless you." This missionary was going through a lot at the time, and every chance I got, I would encourage her and let her know that God loved her and I did, too. When I left that state, she presented me with a Bible saying, "Thank you for not changing and always encouraging me." This change of heart spoke volumes to me. What if I had acted the way she acted toward me? I would have killed my witness, and God would not have been glorified.

Thank God for favor and steadfastness that keeps us from losing our testimony in the midst of the storm. I had to seek God and stay humble while I was going through my period of persecution for right living. "In all things shewing thyself a pattern of good works: in doctrine shewing uncorruptness, gravity, sincerity, sound speech, that cannot be condemned; that he that is of the contrary part may be ashamed, having no evil thing to say of you" (Titus 2:7-8). This verse means that in everything I do, I should make sure to show patterns of good works so that my enemy will see and be made ashamed because of my right living. "Blessed are ye, when men shall revile you, and persecute you, and shall say all manner of evil against you falsely, for my sake" (Matthew 5:11).

Dressing for Battle

How many of you out there have let your guard down because you became familiar with the people at the church you joined? While going through everyday life, you began to leave your armor at home because you felt that you had relationships with those who were all on the same level as you. Everybody was happy for each other, and no one wanted to see anyone else fail. You were one big, happy family. You had all your sisters and brothers with you, and you felt like nothing could ever go wrong.

Does God allow certain experiences to come into our lives to get us on the right track and to make sure we are aligned with His plan? Do we love only those who love us, like the hypocrites do (Luke 6:32)? Many times, I have seen good relationships go bad without any notice, and I wondered if maybe some people are in our lives for a season only.

As Christ suffered in the flesh, we have to arm ourselves likewise. "Yea, and all that will live godly in Christ Jesus shall suffer persecution" (2 Timothy 3:12). Every day is not going to be a bed of roses, but you can keep going. "The weapons of our warfare are not carnal, but mighty through God to the pulling down of strong holds" (2 Corinthians 10:4). No matter what we suffer, we can persevere with the help of the Lord.

"We wrestle not against flesh and blood" (Ephesians 6:12). Although not all mental disorders are demonic in origin, demons sometimes cause physical disease or mental suffering. Demons tempt people into immoral practices. Demons are committed to do evil; God will use them to accomplish His plan during the end of the age (Revelation 16:14). When you are dressed to follow Jesus, many things will happen, but you must know what to do at the appointed time. The Bible admonishes us to "put on the whole armour of God, that ye may be able to stand against the wiles of the devil" (Ephesians 6:11). We must be dressed with humility and clothed with righteousness in order to get through tough times.

A Need for Deliverance

In the midst of all the hurts I have experienced through the years, God has given me a few messages that not only set me free but set others free as well. One particular message God gave me was that I needed a private deliverance. My Scripture came from Mark 5:21-30, where a woman had been dealing with an issue for twelve long years; she spent all she had and did not get better. Can you imagine dealing with something for a long time, yet you think: *What is the use? Everyone else appears to be doing great, but I am dealing with one issue.* I view issues as proceeding from a source, as a consequence or a result of something. God gave me three points regarding the Scripture in Mark.

One point is that our issues isolate us. The woman with the issue of blood could not tell Jesus publicly what was wrong as others did, and therefore she wished for a private cure. How many people within the house of God have issues, but cannot tell anybody what troubles them? A lot of times we ask people for the truth, but sometimes we cannot handle the truth. Therefore, we have to be careful about telling folk when we have private issues, because no one wants to share an issue only to find out later that the issue has made headlines for the gossip column. Whatever you suffer in life, don't let the devil isolate you from the saints. Our inheritance is among sanctified believers, but everyone in the church building is not sanctified.

Once Christ has made you free, you must "stand fast therefore in the liberty wherewith Christ hath made us free, and be not entangled again with the yoke of bondage" (Galatians 5:1). Don't allow your issue to keep binding you, hindering your progress in God. "If the Son therefore shall make you free, ye shall be free indeed" (John 8:36). If God's Son has set you free, you are free; don't let a devil in hell bind you. Deal with your issue, and seek deliverance from God.

My second point is that desperation caused motivation. The Bible declares that the woman with the issue of blood made up her mind to touch Christ's garment (v. 28). In other words, she started talking to herself, telling herself that she had been dealing with this issue long enough. Desperate people do desperate things, and desperation can cause you to break customs and traditions, I know that someone who is reading this book feels the same way; you have been dealing with your issue long enough. When you get in a desperate state, the Spirit of God inside of you will motivate you to keep going and not give up. Having the Holy Ghost as our leader and guide, our present help in the time of trouble, is so important. The Holy Ghost is our *paraclete* (the Greek word for helper) when we feel like we cannot go on. We must always remember that the greater one is inside us (1 John 4:4). Satan's job is to take us out with our issues, but the Holy Ghost is our enabler that motivates us to keep going and not give up.

My third point is that the woman in Mark dealt with the issues for a long period of time. This part is what gets most of us in trouble. We are living in a microwave society, and we want everything done instantaneously. We have a stressful time dealing with things for twelve days, let alone twelve years. If God takes longer than thirty days to move on our behalf, we feel as if He has forgotten about us. At this place in our lives, God's will and purpose for our individual lives are aborted because we are anxious. The Bible says that we should "be careful [anxious] for nothing" (Philippians 4:6). Regardless of what kind of issues you have had to endure in your life, you must remember that God has given you a testimony to share with others about His faithfulness towards you in your time of despair. Could you imagine being hurt and needing a miracle that only God can give? We must always remember that Jesus is a miracle-worker; He is the Great Physician, the wheel in the middle of the wheel (Ezekiel 1:16), and our Great Deliverer. We must do what the woman with the issue of blood did and say, "I won't leave here the way I came, in Jesus' name."

When you come to grips with yourself about your issue, then you can be healed. Denial is a trick the enemy uses to keep us bound by our issues. As we pour our hearts out to God, He can heal the dark, hidden places that we don't always reveal to Him. I admonish everyone that reads this book not to let your issues cause you to doubt God. We must learn to stop masking our issues and let God give us a private deliverance in a public place. Everyone in church does not have to know why you are shouting, but know that the Son has set you free from some things. After you get through your issues, do you still have joy?

Prayer of Confession

Some experiences that I have encountered caused me to whisper many prayers to God. I would like to share with you a prayer that I wrote on August 10, 2003. "Lord, I am naked before You, and nothing is hid or covered from You. I need You, Father, and I am at a point of decision. I am not happy with the way things are done at the church I attend. I have sat and observed the way things are done in Your house, and I am grieved because of how sickening things are. I know You are there, God, but You must have a better way than what we have experienced thus far. We need divine intervention now, please don't let us fall in the Spirit. Lord, help us keep our eyes on You. We need Your direction; I am tired of things being out of order in Your house. I know You to be a God of excellence and of order. Help me to look to You and wait until You give me what to do. I am willing to do Your will that we might be free in You, in Jesus' name. Amen."

Needing a Break

Have you ever been so overwhelmed that you felt you needed a break from everything and everybody? In October 2004, I needed a break, and I wrote a letter to God, saying: "Dear Lord, I thank You for allowing me to take a break this weekend. I plan to get intimate with You. Lord, I want to rekindle the fire that we once had. I want to revive my relationship with You. I seek this weekend Your direction for me and my life. I don't want to waste any more time. I want to be reacquainted with You this weekend. Help me, Father, to look to You and to allow this weekend to be a renewing; let it be one of the best weekends of my life. Everything You have prepared for me this weekend, please give it to me. I need the strength to endure and to move forward in life with confidence."

I wrote this note at a time when I felt overwhelmed in church. I had my own problems, and every time I looked around, someone was telling me his or her problems. Many times, I could barely maintain trying to handle my trials, but one day the idea of taking a break came to me. I asked my husband whether he minded if I flew to Chicago for five days to take a break. He was okay with me taking that time off to rest and hear from God. When I mentioned my trip to people in church, I was told that God would not tell a woman to go out of town without her husband to take a break.

During this time, I was working full-time, going to college full-time, and taking care of my two sons. Also, my mother-in-law was in a coma for two months, and every day I went to the hospital, sometimes two or three times a day. This accumulating stress was my life from June until August. When my mother-in-law died, I was distraught, and I took her passing very hard, although I knew she was in a better place, because we were close. I really think I was getting ready to have a nervous breakdown. My body held up long enough for me to get on the plane and check into the hotel. In the baggage claim, I met a lady who said that the Lord told her to tell me that during the weekend He was going to give me much wisdom. I went to my room and slept for twelve hours the first night. The next day, I slept thirteen hours. I was mentally and physically drained.

Although some folks did not understand my situation, my body was talking to me saying, "Take a break." I took myself to dinner, went to a spa, and got a massage. I walked the mall and bought a few items, but I did not once receive the wisdom that I was told God would give me. When I checked out of the hotel, I got on the plane, and I could not understand what had happened to me. I felt rested, but I had not received much wisdom yet.

When I got back to Anchorage, people started pulling on me again to volunteer for various tasks, and I told them no. I started telling people that my schedule was too busy to take on additional tasks right now and that I had to do what was best for me. Immediately, I realized that I had received much wisdom; I had learned how to say no and not to overtax myself. This break was the beginning of realizing that saying no is not a sin, although church folks can make you feel like you have sinned because you are not overtaxed and burned-out. I started to understand that God wants my best, and I don't have to have a full schedule to give Him my best. I like closure. Whatever task God is giving me, I need to make sure that He is my focus, not man. People will overtax you if you let them and if you are not careful.

Don't Be Bitter

When people tell me how I should not allow hurt to bother me, I find their opinion comical. Sometimes, I do not feel that we think about the things we say to hurting people. When you are going through difficulty, church folks quote Scriptures with authority and then tell you to pray. They forget to tell you that, when they prayed about their situations, God did not show up for a while. They cried, complained, and wanted everyone to feel sorry for them. Why the standard different when you or I hurt? As you wait on God and seek direction from Him, you see the enemy trying to kill your character, working overtime with those who oppose you to make sure that you will not be anything in their church or any other church if they can help it. How do you handle life when church folks have gotten together and come up with a Scripture to justify their wrongdoing? What do you do when you are mistreated and folks threaten you, saying that God is going to get you for bothering them? I know that many of you reading this book have the same questions in your mind that I have had for years.

God is love, and He wants all of us to love one another. No matter how hard things get, we must show love to one another and cast our cares upon the Lord, who cares for us (1 Peter 5:7). My grandmother used to say about God that He may not come when you want Him, but He is always on time. How do you handle the stress and disappointment that comes with living a holy life and knowing that your adversary is sitting beside you in the pew or standing beside you taking communion? God must help us.

I remember a mother who told me once that, regardless of what anyone else does, I must make sure that I keep my heart pure. Don't let the wrongdoing of others cause you to become bitter and have a hard heart. That advice spoke volumes to me, because this woman spoke to me during a time when I was accused of taking over a church, when all I did was speak under the anointing. I was shocked that someone would think something like that. I felt as if someone had stabbed me in my heart, knowing that church folks thought that I would stoop to that level.

I was in the midst of a YPWW (Young People Willing Workers) session one time when an elder yelled at me and said, "You don't know everything, Evangelist!" All I was doing was answering a question, and everyone in the class looked at me. But the Holy Ghost in me would not let me retaliate. I refused to fight with the people of God. I bowed out gracefully and let peace abide. No matter what people have done to me through the years, the God in me taught me how to humble myself and give all offenses to Him. Sometimes I felt like retaliating, but I did not get saved in order to fight my brothers or sisters. I've been hurt by friendly fire more times than I care to name, but God sustained me in the midst of everything. I am forever living the Scripture of giving no offense in anything so that the ministry will not be blamed (2 Corinthians 6:3).

A few days later in another setting, I was told that I was not saved and had never been saved. I sat still with a smile on my face, knowing that God would vindicate me in His own time. "For I know that my redeemer liveth" (Job 19:25) inside of me. I know who I am, and as the world did not give me salvation, I cannot let the world cause me to give up on what God has begun in me. Many times, I have had to "endure hardness, as a good soldier" (2 Timothy 2:3); I took the persecution that I received for being anointed. I never knew that the anointing could bring so much opposition. I would hear my fellow ministers in the gospel say words like: "You think you are so anointed; you do not have a monopoly on God." This accusation was so far from the truth, because the foundation that I received was built on prayer, fasting, and studying God's Word.

The pastor of my church at the time would always admonish me not to get up before God's people without the anointing. I cried many days, because I was afraid to speak God's Word without the anointing; therefore, I fasted, prayed, and consecrated myself so that God could show up and I could hear from Him. Believe me when I say that I count myself least of them all. I was raised in the South, at a time when everyone around me had little or no ambition to become something great. At a young age, I had determined that I would be somebody great and that God had more for me than what I had seen growing up in the South. My desire was that God would preserve me and not let me grow up only to have nothing happen to me. I went to college for eighteen months after high school as an avenue to leave home. I had a burning desire to succeed in life and not to live a life of shame and regret. The most important thing that I did in life was accepting Christ. I gave God my heart and asked Him to use me however He chose.

I never knew that, once I became a broken and yielded vessel, God would pour Himself out on me in so many special ways. I must confess that I have cried and asked God why He gave me a gift that causes so much jealousy and mistreatment? I have come to realize that people will focus on the gift and not the giver of the gift. God anointed me, and I find it strange that church folk do not celebrate His gift. Some of my trials have caused me to take a step back, but I refuse to be like Naomi. She was a prime example of how trials, tribulation, and hurt can cause someone to become bitter, as we see in Ruth 1:20: "And she said unto them, Call me not Naomi, call me Mara: for the Almighty hath dealt very bitterly with me." Naomi left the place that God had visited in Moab and returned back to Bethlehem in Judah, a place which was familiar. After she lost her husband and sons, she felt that surely God was against her, because of her losses and her great trials.

Although her heart was hurt, she could not see God in the midst of her pain and hurt. Naomi says in Ruth 1:21, "I went out full, and the LORD hath brought me home again empty: why then call ye me Naomi, seeing the LORD hath testi-

fied against me, and the Almighty hath afflicted me?" Naomi
believed that God had sent her back empty and had afflicted
her. We can definitely relate this belief to our present life
situations. How many times has life appeared as if God's
hand was against us, and how many times have we failed to
see the blessings of God all around us?

Naomi let her hurts make her bitter, but I do not believe
that this response is the will of God for us. Our hurts and
disappointments should make us better! Tribulations come
to make us strong. Although we cannot always see this
benefit in the midst of our dilemmas, I dare anyone reading
this book to trust God and have faith that He is working out
your trials for your good. What you are enduring does not
feel, taste, sound, look, or smell good, but God is working
it out for your good. What the devil means for evil, God
turns around to use for our good. How many times have you
thought your trial was going to take you out of God's favor
or notice, but late in the midnight hour, God turned it around
to start working in your favor? Those that lied about you
and ostracized you and tried to kill your influence ended up
needing your help. And the Holy Ghost in you caused you to
do the right thing.

Forget about what others say, because the Holy Ghost
requires us to show love in spite of what we suffer. Thank
God for the love of God that "constraineth us" (2 Corinthians
5:14). I can truly say that if not for the mercies of God, I would
have been consumed (Lamentations 3:22). Many times, I

wanted to get my own revenge, because God appeared to be taking too long and the enemy was having a field day with my feelings and good name. However, God stepped in right on time and snatched my name out of the mouth of the enemy, and the same tongue that used to curse me blesses me now that God has changed their speech.

Know Your Purpose

My sole purpose in life is to praise and worship God and to declare His word. God created me to do this work, and anything outside of it throws me off. I have to bless Him at all times, because I know what not feeling His presence yet wanting God more than my necessary food is like. I know what reading His Word, weeping, and thinking about how merciful He is towards me is like. I have experienced the hand of God in the midst of my most difficult trials, yet He takes time to speak a word to me, in my season.

I remember crying out to God about what church folks were doing; I said, "Lord, how long do I have to put up with this mistreatment? There is a church on every corner." The Lord told me verbally, "I will prove My Spirit in you, but I will not prove your flesh." That Ramah word spoke volumes to me, just to know that God was going to prove that His spirit was abiding in me, and no devil in hell could change that reassurance. Knowing that God was going to turn the situation around gave me hope and peace in God. Not many days from the day God spoke to me, He turned the situation around, and those that plotted to do me harm ended up doing me good. And the Spirit of God convicted them and caused them to apologize. God has a way of uncovering the plan of the enemy.

Many observers stood by and witnessed the various trials I encountered, and when those trials were all over, I could look back to say that all I endured was worthwhile. Just to feel God's presence and to be anointed the more was worth every bit of persecution I received, because God was glorified at the end. "Weeping may endure for a night, but joy cometh in the morning" (Psalm 30:5). Had I known that the anointing that God had put on me was going to be so great, I believe I could have stayed in the fire a little while longer. No matter what you are suffering, remember that you must do what God has called you to do and let Him take care of your enemies. Your hope is in your calling. "I tell you that he will avenge them speedily. Nevertheless when the Son of man cometh, shall he find faith on the earth?" (Luke 18:8).

Spirit of Distraction

You will hear me saying often that, if I am going through a trial, then God is trying to work something in or out of me. The irony is that God the Father knows just how much we can bear. The enemy brings the spirit of distraction to get our focus off what God has created us to do. If the enemy can leave us broken-down, hurt, bitter, angry, and in a place of isolation, then he has us where he wants us. But God has given us everything we need that pertains to life and godliness (2 Peter 1:3). I remember one evangelist who always said, "Keep your eyes on Jesus." At that time, as a new convert, I did not understand the phrase, but by and by it became clear to me.

Now that I am older, I see clearly what she was saying. No matter what distractions come our way, our eyes must stay focused on the Lord. If we take our eyes off God, then we, like Peter, will begin to sink. No matter how loud the growl of the enemy is, and the Bible declares that he is like a roaring lion seeking whom he may devour (1 Peter 5:8), we do not have to give him permission to devour us. Trials are going to come, but stay focused, "looking unto Jesus the author and finisher of our faith" (Hebrews 12:2). In the midst of our trials, we must have a tunnel vision that sees only what God is saying to us about the situation or about ourselves.

When God is not talking, then we must keep praying and waiting for an answer. Someone wrote a song once which says that the safest place in the whole wide world is in the will of God. Our lives will not always be on the mountain peak, but wherever we might be, God is in control of our lives. Sometimes, you must take a step back and ask God to give you clear direction and to order your steps according to His Word. Doing so is not always easy, but it is necessary. If most of us would be honest, staying focused is easier said than done. I thought to myself before: *How can I stay focused when everything around me is falling apart? How can I focus when people who love me and think they are doing me a favor by reminding me of what I am suffering keep on rehearsing my pain?* I sometimes have to walk away from everything and everybody in order to hear from God what He is truly saying to me. Many times, I have found myself writing down my thoughts, because I cannot tell them to anyone but God.

I thank God for never leaving me or forsaking me, even in the midst of my pain and trouble. Some ways I found helpful in staying focused were listening to spiritually uplifting songs, absorbing preaching that spoke to my situation, praying, and fasting. Taking the time to fast for your own flesh can be rewarding. The more you deny your flesh, the better control you will have over it. Every saint must bring his body under subjection to the Spirit of God. Letting the flesh know that praise is not an option in the midst of a trial it is mandatory. I make myself do what is right, and I find myself worshipping God through the storm. My best worship is in the midst of my trials, for at that place I recognize the awesomeness of God and the love He has shown to the children of men.

In worship, I meet the Father and commune with Him, letting Him know that I love Him. Worship causes me to become desperate for God, having the right attitude and realizing that I need Him and cannot keep going without His presence. At this place of dependence, God shows up and gives relief from the burdens. I am cognizant of the fact that He knows just how much I can bear. In worship, I feel like no one else is on the face of the earth but me and God. So much security, safety, and peace are in the presence of my Father. My Father helps me in both small and great trials. I understand clearly what David meant in Psalm 51:11: "Cast me not away from thy presence; and take not thy holy spirit from me." David understood that, no matter what he had done wrong, he could not survive without the Spirit of the almighty God. If he was going to experience any peace or consolation in what he had to suffer, he needed God's Spirit to abide with him. Trying to maintain life in this world without the Spirit of God is like a man taking a walk on a long journey alone.

Pit to Purpose

In the Bible, Joseph had a dream, but the haters could not stand the fact that God was going to make him successful. His brothers tried to stop his destiny and the divine purpose of God. Their act of selling him into slavery was part of God's plan to get Joseph from the pit to the palace. We have to know that, even in our pit, God can still orchestrate the plan to move us to the place that He has promised. God has a way of turning things around when we are in the midst of the storm; when night seems to enclose us, I must say that God is working in our favor. What the devil meant for bad, God meant for Joseph's good. The kind of God we serve will not allow the enemy to triumph over us.

No matter whom the devil uses, God is in control, and He is the devil's boss. While reading this book, I pray that you will start looking at some of those pits where you are trapped and some that you have escaped and know that you are positioned for a purpose. If we could take the hurt and pain and use those tests and trials as a means to climb to the next level, God would be glorified. Your pit might be different from mine, but know that God is the One who turns things around. He works hard to validate His chosen people.

The Father did not just save us because He needed something to do; every step we take should line up with God's plan and purpose. The Bible declares in Psalm 37:23 that "the steps of a good man are ordered by the Lord." You might not understand what you are suffering, but know that your steps are ordered by the Lord. Who can stop the plan of God? He has a way of working all things after the counsel of His own will (Ephesians 1:11). Nothing just happens to those who are blood-washed by the power of God. What I like about God is that He does not have to get permission from our enemies to lift us out of the pit and bring us to His purpose. All He needs is for us to trust Him to do what only God can do. Before the foundation of the world, God had already laid out a plan for our lives. As God had a purpose for Jeremiah, so He has a purpose for each of us. Before Jeremiah was born, God knew him, sanctified him, determined that he should be a prophet, and set him apart for the office(Jeremiah 1:4-9).

God never intended for us to wander around aimlessly, trying on our own to figure out where we belong, but God created us to glorify Him. People, do not allow you being young to hinder you from obeying God; the Bible says, "I will pour out my spirit upon all flesh; and your sons and your daughters shall prophesy, your old men shall dream dreams, your young men shall see visions" (Joel 2:28). You might not understand what you are going through, but "we know that all things work together for good to them that love God, to them who are the called according to his purpose" (Romans 8:28). I thank God, "Who hath saved us, and called us with an holy calling, not according to our works, but according to his own purpose and grace, which was given us in Christ Jesus before the world began" (2 Timothy 1:9). God has a purpose for each one of us. We were created in His image to bless His name. God will call us to that purpose for which He has designed us, for His purposes cannot be frustrated.

Faithful until Death

Faithfulness comes from a root meaning to be permanent, secure, and reliable. From this word comes the associated idea of genuine faith. Believers need to be faithful in our lives and service to God. A lot of times, we get into trouble because of what we are enduring for a season. We know the right thing to do, but because of our circumstances or situations, we choose not to obey because doing so is an inconvenience to those who are faithful to God during this time. We spend too much time justifying why we are not doing what we are supposed to do.

Like Jeremiah, I look at the faithfulness of God towards me. "It is of the LORD's mercies that we are not consumed, because his compassions fail not. They are new every morning: great is thy faithfulness. The LORD is my portion, saith my soul; therefore will I hope in him" (Lamentations 3:22-24). This statement of faith right here is enough to make anyone rejoice for a while. Hebrews 10:23 says, "Let us hold fast the profession of our faith without wavering; (for he is faithful that promised)." Job was a biblical example of someone who was committed to God's will. Although Job did not understand where or why he was suffering, he was confident enough to say that "though he slay me, yet will I trust in him" (Job 13:15). We must understand that real faithfulness is more than inner belief, even more than whole-soul commitment. Real faithfulness is a condition of the soul marked by such a stable character and an attitude of total trust that the believer's life is inspired with consistent, responsible service to God.

Why Sit You Here and Die?

The Bible talks about four lepers sitting outside of a city. Any one of us can put ourselves in their situation, where they were isolated and dying in a place of stagnation, while going to church week after week. The lepers had a problem, and they decided just to sit still and die. But then the lepers asked the question that I am going to ask those who are reading this book: "Why sit we here until we die?" (2 Kings 7:3). Please tell me why you are letting pain, hurt, and disappointment handicap you to the point of dying? You cannot change the past, but the fact that you lived through the hurt long enough to read this book should encourage you to go on. I know how you feel when you are trying to get over one hurt and, before you know it, you are getting hurt again. You did not have enough time to heal from the first trial. You didn't even have time to take a breath when here come something else.

Do not sit there in the midst of all of that hurt and die. Do as the lepers decided to do; get up, go into the enemy camp, and take back your peace, joy, and happiness. Don't give anybody that much control over you. I believe that these lepers did not have names because you or I could easily put ourselves in their place. You must be willing to take a chance and believe that God is with you and that He is concerned about everything you suffer. Step out in God, my brothers and sisters, and trust Him. You must make up your mind that whatever happens, happens because you refuse to sit still and die. Some of us are in situations where we are dying spiritually, and we are wondering how we are going to endure. Your situation might have caused you to be isolated from the saints, but you know that you need something from God. You realize that, if you sit there in that hurt, disappointment, and discouragement, you might die. Maybe you need to do what the lepers did and tell yourself that you are not going to sit there and die. I am not going to close my mouth and refuse to praise God because of my circumstances and situations.

Regardless of what is going on around you, God is still worthy; in the midst of your trial, He is worthy. We have to get that Queen Esther attitude, "So will I go in unto the king … and if I perish, I perish" (Esther 4:16). Like Esther, say, "I cannot sit here in my situation and watch myself die. God is the life-giver, and He said that He will allow no temptation to come upon you that He will not give you a means of escape or a way to bear" (1 Corinthians 10:13). You might be sick, lonely in a bad marriage, or in a situation that you cannot seem to shake, but you have to do what the woman with the issue of blood did and just touch the hem of His garment so that you will be made whole. "We have not an high priest which cannot be touched with the feeling of our infirmities; but was in all points tempted like as we are, yet without sin" (Hebrews 4:15). Make up your mind that you are refusing to die in that hurt. Declare God's word: "I shall not die, but live, and declare the works of the LORD" (Psalm 118:17).

Glad I Know Him!

Paul said, "That I may know him, and the power of his resurrection, and the fellowship of his sufferings, being made conformable unto his death" (Philippians 3:10). Some of the experiences that I have had in the church left me baffled, wondering: *What is going on with the standards of holiness and why has the love of many waxed cold (Matthew 24:12)? If God is love and His very nature is love, then how can we operate as ambassadors of Christ without love?* Doing so is contrary to what the Scriptures declare. One of my favorite passages is "But God commendeth his love toward us, in that, while we were yet sinners, Christ died for us" (Romans 5:8). This Scripture keeps me going in tough times, reminding me that Jesus sacrificed His life for many. I have been in situations where folks act like they, not Jesus, died for my sins, and they tried to hold their self-righteousness over my head. But I thank God that no one can make me doubt Him, for I know too much about Him.

Sometimes, when you are dealing with so much at one time, you become distracted, and if you are not careful, you will lose your focus. I have cried many nights because of being wronged by others. I wanted so badly to vindicate myself, but God would not let me. My heart was heavy, but I held my peace and let the Lord fight my battle. Most of the pain and hurt that I have encountered through the years was in the church. I think that I expected haters in the world, but in the place that is called the house of God, I never expected so much pain. Now I understand what Jesus was saying when He said, "But I have prayed for thee, that thy faith fail not" (Luke 22:32). "Many are the afflictions of the righteous: but the LORD delivereth him out of them all" (Psalm 34:19). Sometimes I wonder if people know who they are dealing with when they lie about me and persecute me. I am a child of the highest God, the apple of His eye, and whoever touches me touches Him. I am God's choice, and I did not choose myself. Therefore, I cannot succumb to the tactics of the enemy. I have a God to glorify, and I must spend my time doing the will of the Lord. The enemy wants me to give up and throw in the towel, but it is too late, because I know in whom I believe.

I did not get saved in order to fight church folks and to deal with jealousy and the different spirits that attack the anointing that God places on an individual. Why is showing love and being doers of the Word (James 1:22) so hard for church folks to do? The product on the market, Jesus Christ the righteous, is the best, but His representation is poor. Because of immaturity, our churches have handicapped, crippled, and thrown away so many people that had great potential. The old mothers used to say, "If you do not know what you are doing, leave well enough alone." Do not damage people, because you never know if you will get another opportunity to fix what you have messed up.

Throughout my Christian journey, I have seen some bold, disobedient church folks who name the name of Christ but refuse to humble themselves for the sake of Christ. Their pride level is so high that these people would rather see others die and go to hell than to come off their arrogant horse to witness or to say that they are sorry for their wrongdoing. This kind of attitude is definitely not the true Spirit of Jesus Christ, who died that we all might have life (John 10:10). You don't know who God has put in your path to bless you, and a lot of us abort the plan of God by looking at things in the flesh. We focus on ourselves and become "lovers of pleasures more than lovers of God" (2 Timothy 3:4). In the Bible, Jesus declares that "they that are whole have no need of the physician, but they that are sick: I came not to call the righteous, but sinners to repentance" (Mark 2:17). We cannot throw anyone away, because the Bible says to "judge nothing before the time" (1 Corinthians 4:5). A lot of things people are discarding and pushing to the side, God is elevating and anointing for His service. When you are God's choice, you don't have to play politics or mind games to get to the top, because your gift will make room for you.

My spirit is grieved when I see folks that God has anointed sell their souls to the devil for a position or in order to be in the limelight for a few minutes. Do we not know that if man put you up, man can take you down? "The blessing of the LORD, it maketh rich, and he addeth no sorrow with it" (Proverbs 10:22). Why are saints looking for validation in all the wrong places? We only set ourselves up to be hurt over and over again. "Lift up your heads, O ye gates; and be ye lift up, ye everlasting doors; and the King of glory shall come in" (Psalm 24:7). Stop giving mere man all this power to control you and your destiny. Where I say you can go or what I say you can be does not matter. What is the Master's plan for you? You should be seeking the Master to make sure that you are lining up with His will and purpose for your individual life. "Many are the afflictions of the righteous; but the LORD delivereth him out of them all" (Psalm 34:19). We can trust God in the midst of the hurt and pain and know that He is in control.

We must learn to trust Him even when we cannot find the strength to trust Him.

Joy comes from the inside of me when I think of the Master's plan for my life, and that God "hath made him to be sin for us, who knew no sin; that we might be made the righteousness of God in him" (2 Corinthians 5:21). Why do we meet some people who act like they are the ones who died on the cross for our transgressions? They are self-righteous, and they spend countless hours trying to prove their point or character. Jesus paid it all, and all to Him we owe. We don't owe each other anything but love; and self-exaltation is the very vice that keeps us from reaching those levels in God that He has for us. Many nights, I have cried over the hurts inflicted by church folks, but "thanks be unto God, which always causeth us to triumph in Christ, and maketh manifest the savour of his knowledge by us in every place" (2 Corinthians 2:14). I can truly say, "If it had not been the LORD who was on our side, when men rose up against us: Then they had swallowed us up quick, when their wrath was kindled against us" (Psalm 124:2-3). Only the grace and mercy of God caused me to keep going when I felt like giving up. So many times, my flesh wanted to quit and felt that the end was not worth the pain, but the Spirit said, "Go ahead."

Bitterness to Blindness

B itterness can blind you; if you are not careful, you will find yourself nursing wounds of unforgivenss, hatred, and jealousy. The Bible says that "if the blind lead the blind, both shall fall into the ditch" (Matthew 15:14). We cannot teach people how to get delivered until we have been delivered. Jesus taught by precept and example.

There is a place in God that will remove all hurt and pain. When you really have a mind to please God, your focus will be on Him, not on the actions of those who are immature and do not have the mind of God. As I travel throughout the United States, I constantly meet people who have been hurt by people in the church. Hurt does not have a specific name or brand assigned to it, and no one is immune to pain. Hurt comes in all races, genders, and cultures. My working definition of hurt is pain that grips your heart or body caused by an individual or as a result of a situation.

Everyone has or will experience pain at one time or another in life. Sometimes, the pain you experience can cause you to take a step back and catch your breath in order to survive. I cannot tell anyone how much pain he is able to bear, because only the Father knows just how much we can bear. Others may downplay your hurts, but I am glad that "we have not an high priest which cannot be touched with the feeling of our infirmities; but was in all points tempted like as we are, yet without sin" (Hebrews 4:15). "The sufferings of this present time are not worthy to be compared with the glory which shall be revealed in us" (Romans 8:18). We can talk about the glory to come all day long, but now we must live and deal with our hurts. I am finding out that, as God brings me out of trials, I could bear more than I realized. "Many are the afflictions of the righteous: but the LORD delivereth him out of them all" (Psalm 34:19).

Many people bury pain and hurt, but as my grandmother used to say, "If you bury something that is alive, it will eventually work its way back to the top." With hurt comes the pain associated with a betrayal, disappointment, or misunderstanding. Hurt can attack a person's mental state, physical health, and trust and confidence level. I view hurt as a tool that can make a person bitter or better. This tool is designed to make us strong, for the Bible declares in Romans 5:3-5 that "we glory in tribulations also: knowing that tribulation worketh patience; and patience, experience; and experience, hope: and hope maketh not ashamed; because the love of God is shed abroad in our hearts by the Holy Ghost which is given unto us." Knowing that God is with us in the midst of every trial makes life better.

I am grateful that God will never leave or forsake me. Many people mask their hurts through makeup, clothing, or joking, but whatever is inside a person will come out of him in some way. Trying to mask hurts reminds me of when the crowd told Peter when he denied Jesus that his speech betrayed him (Matthew 26:73). When hurt has allowed a person to become bitter, his speech betrays him. Even if you try to cover up the pain by saying all the right things and making sure that you are politically correct, hurt will still reveal the true heart of a person. I am persuaded that a lot of hurts that people encounter in the church come from a lack of maturity, jealousy, unforgiveness, and insecurity. All the things I mention come out of an undelivered vessel. God has given us all things pertaining to life and godliness (2 Peter 1:3), and we must yield ourselves to God totally. No matter how well a person can preach or teach, deliverance must come from time to time. Emotions and intellect alone are not enough to keep you from hurting people or being hurt.

We need Jesus to be Lord over our lives, and every now and then we need to holler, "Master, save me!" As Paul says, "Walk in the Spirit, and ye shall not fulfil the lust of the flesh" (Galatians 5:16) and offend those whom we are supposed to love. Those that live by the flesh will die by the flesh. Jesus knew His mission and did not deviate from it; He was not distracted by fame, popularity, or arrogance. Jesus even said, "The Son of man is come to seek and to save that which was lost" (Luke 19:10). We must re-identify why we are in the church and what our purpose is. The Bible declares, "Ye are our epistle written in our hearts, known and read of all men" (2 Corinthians 3:2); ask yourself if your video is matching your audio. If not, then something is wrong; we should strive daily to be less like ourselves and more like Jesus. People want to see the love of Christ radiating from us on a daily basis. The Bible tells us to "let God be true, but every man a liar" (Romans 3:4). When we put our confidence in man, we are headed for heartaches and disappointments. The disappointment that comes from hurt is normally prefaced by a confidence or trust placed in an individual other than God.

The Bible admonishes that we should be people who "have no confidence in the flesh" (Philippians 3:3). Many of our various trials are designed to push us toward God and away from mere men. We have total control over what we say and to whom we say it. I have met many people that were wounded to the point of no return by church folks. I must ask: how can those of us who name the name of Christ with a clear conscience willfully cause others to stumble?

I have met people that were wrong and knew it but were not willing to change for the sake of the gospel. The soul did not matter, because pride was at work. I cannot think of any thing or situation that I have encountered that would cause me to attack the people of God. "For unto whomsoever much is given, of him shall be much required: and to whom men have committed much, of him they will ask the more" (Luke 12:48). Paul warns us that the wrath of God is revealed from heaven against all ungodliness and unrighteousness of men, who hold the truth in unrighteousness (Romans 1:18). The Bible declares that "every idle word that men shall speak, they shall give account thereof in the day of judgment" (Matthew 12:36). I don't think that many people take this Scripture literally, because they do and say whatever they want and feel justified doing so.

They answer to no man, because they carry titles and have positions. Some feel that this authority gives them the right to talk to God's chosen people wrongly and to keep shouting and preaching. The Bible says, "Many will say to me in that day, Lord, Lord, have we not prophesied in thy name? and in thy name have cast out devils? and in thy name done many wonderful works? And then will I profess unto them, I never knew you: depart from me, ye that work iniquity" (Matthew 7:22-23). I pray that this book will not only inspire those who have been hurt by someone who professed salvation but will also convict those who are the cause of many hurting people. "Woe unto the world because of offences! For it must needs be that offences come; but woe to that man by who the offence cometh!" (Matthew 18:7).

I have been in the ministry for twenty years, and I am convinced that some people just went. They did not wait on God to call, qualify, and justify, as their actions make evident. Their ministry is not centered on soul-winning but on people-bashing. They have the attitude: "What can I do to make others look bad while I look good in the eyes of the people?" Regardless of how badly I hurt, past, present, and future, I must forgive and love in spite of everything. I remember a mother who always encouraged me to let nothing get in my heart, when people do mean things to me. Those mothers went through a lot, and they are now matriarchs in today's society. Much of what I suffer, I chalk up as experience, trusting that God is working something in or out of me. The love and compassion He puts in me for my offenders is amazing to me. I find myself praying for them and asking God for mercy and help for them, because I truly do not want the devil to have anybody. I have never been the type that could hold grudges, and people that know me will tell you that I normally get things off of my chest quick.

During some seasons in our lives, God will not allow us to get things off our chest, because He wants to be glorified in the midst of what we are suffering. I have learned how to hold my peace and truly let the Lord fight my battle, but I am amazed at how people can do you wrong and then threaten to tell God on you as if you were not His child also. The beauty of all of this difficulty is that God is merciful and He is not finished with us yet. For this reason alone, you can "love your enemies, bless them that curse you, do good to them that hate you, and pray for them which despitefully use you, and persecute you" (Matthew 5:44). Doing so has not always been easy for me, but I had to grow into this ability in order to stay free from the various trials that came my way.

Sometimes I think it would be nice for Jesus to do as he did with the woman caught in adultery and say, "He that is without sin among you, let him first cast a stone at her" (John 8:7). That crowd then is no different from the crowd today, an arrogant, crooked, and perverse nation that lacks compassion and is full of self-righteousness. How soon we forget the place from which God has actually brought us! Our forgetfulness is sad but true, and some of us are still there. We have not moved from the place of rescue to the place of change. For this reason we so easily look down on others while justifying our own wrongdoing. Our God is a God of truth, and He does not deal in half-truths.

Do you realize how many people would be lost if God represented us the way we represent Him? I really don't think many people ever thought about this question, because if we had, we would find a lot more mercy and a little less arrogance and self-righteousness floating throughout our churches. I determined years ago that I am a mercy case, and if it had not been for the mercies of God I would be consumed (Lamentations 3:22). I know for a fact that I need God, and I try to spread His love and compassion throughout the land. I have been hurt and offended many times, but I learn to pick up my heart and my feelings, give the problem to God, and keep going.

I cannot afford to lose my focus as to why I am here. The fact that I am on this earth now is not happenstance. God has a plan and purpose for my life. I feel inspired to write this book because I want others to hear my testimony and see how God has taken many trials and hurts that could have made me bitter, and made me better. I have suffered verbal attack throughout my ministry, yet I trust God and love Him with all my heart. I share the same prayer that Stephen said: "Lord, lay not this sin to their charge" (Acts 7:60). Some of the foolishness I have encountered has caused me to have a greater appreciation of the Holy Spirit inside of me. When you come from a background of hurt and disappointment, giving your heart to anyone is hard because of the fear of being hurt again. I have learned through salvation that we have to give our hearts to Jesus, who will never fail. I try to be cautious when I know that I am dealing with a person that has encountered hurt from within the church. Those people are hard to win back. As the Scripture says, "A brother offended is harder to be won than a strong city" (Proverbs 18:19). If all baptized believers could get the requirement to be like Jesus in their minds, then everything would be all right. Paul said, "I am crucified with Christ: nevertheless I live; yet not I, but Christ liveth in me: and the life which I now live in the flesh I live by the faith of the Son of God, who loved me, and gave himself for me" (Galatians 2:20). If we could allow the Holy Spirit to infiltrate our hearts with the Word of God, we would survive a lot of hard trials and tribulations.

When Christ lives in us, His love should constrain us to do what is right. Mind games and manipulation should never be practiced among us, once we have given our hearts to Jesus. We must daily crucify the flesh and "put on the whole armour of God, that ye may be able to stand against the wiles of the devil" (Ephesians 6:11). I would say that the reason we have a lot of hurt in the church is that we have undelivered people leading and teaching others. How can you teach me to be free when you are bound? "If the blind lead the blind, both shall fall into the ditch" (Matthew 15:14). Those who are undelivered are full of anger and bitterness, and they use as a bashing station the opportunity that they should use to share the Word of God. Flesh operation causes people to run away from the house of God. People who are holding the truth in righteousness should look around to see who they are helping or hurting. Jesus drew people to Him, not away from Him. His actions make a major difference when it comes to our purpose to bring men and women back to Christ. How can anyone who is not displaying the attributes of Christ win someone to Him? In today's society, people want to see something; they hear what we are saying but see what we do. Jesus taught by precept and example, and many followed Him because of the life He lived.

Challenges that Invoke Change

Some of the things we suffer cause us to change the way God would have us be. Suffering is almost like a preparation to ensure that the best comes out of us. Many challenges and situations that Christians encounter honor God. I can put up with a lot of things, because I have been through a lot of challenges in my life. One thing I have learned through the years is how to get up, brush myself off, forgive, and keep going. In my heart, I've determined not to allow anything or anyone to cause me to become bitter and start resenting God and the church. Although I have encountered great hurt from the church, in many cases God used my trials as testimonies. All of us have been hurt at one time or another, and in the midst of reading now some of you are hurt and wondering how you are going to last through the pain. Looking to Jesus is how you are going to last.

Take your eyes off man and the situation, and trust God. We might not understand everything that is going on, but we must trust God to make everything all right. All right is not contingent on how you feel right now; all right is based on where you are going. When this trial is all over, will I be able to tell someone else how He brought me out all right? If you live long enough, folks can teach you how to trust and depend totally on God, through their fickle ways. Truly, no one else is like Jehovah, and I find myself constantly in prayer asking for the mind of Christ. Many days, I desired to disappear off the earth long enough to regroup and collect my thoughts. This desire is definitely a challenge, because my presence is needed in the earth.

In 1995, I can remember going through some challenging events with some sisters in the church. Many times, I felt lonely, but I did not want to get close to anyone because of the instability of the people. I take the Scripture literally that we should do all things heartily as unto the Lord (Colossians 3:23). Everything to which I put my hands appeared to prosper, but the more I saw victory, the more challenges came my way. While cooking one day, I began to think about God and what I was experiencing, and suddenly a voice spoke to me and said, "For a time such as this" (Esther 4:14). Those few words spoke volumes to me, because I began to understand that God had groomed me for a time such as this, to handle the trials that were coming my way. The trials did not go away, but my understanding was quickened. I learned how to stand fast and wait on God to deliver me. I have always been encouraged, and many times God has laid me on people's hearts. Some of the most influential people in my life are still around encouraging me, and many have been helped.

I Am Better

I refuse to let what I go through cause me to be bitter; I charge the atmosphere with praise and command the negative situations in my life to make me better. I silence every lying tongue and demand the enemy of lack to move away from my door. I place a demand on the anointing of God that is prevalent in my life to loose every chain that is trying to bind me and give me the power to shake them off and make the devil take them back. When I look at why I was created, then I should praise God in the good and bad times.

As John said that Jesus needed to go through Samaria (John 4:4), I feel that I needed to go through some difficult places to get to where the Lord would have me to be. Life is not always easy, but I can overcome! I command from the north, south, east, and west peace that surpasses all understanding and everything that the Father has set in motion for me before the foundation of the world. Please take a moment to recognize that I know how to hurt yet stay in the will of God. My determination is to let nothing and nobody separate me from the love of God (Romans 8:39). I am persuaded to love God, and I have been convinced by the great gospel that I have heard for over twenty years.

Jesus my Master is still teaching me how to release the hurts and let them go. Although many would make you think that this kind of healing is an overnight process, I beg to differ. Healing is a continual process, while miracles happen instantaneously. I don't agree with those who think that mental and spiritual hurt will just go away with time. The cliché that time heals all wounds is for physical hurt, not emotional, mental, or spiritual hurts. I used to think that way because of what I had been taught in the past. The emotional scars surface when you least expect them to do so, and those wounds are deep. God is the only source that can truly heal hurts, emotions, mental and spiritual hurts.

My Prayer for You

My prayer is that every hurt you have encountered throughout your life will be released from you as you go through the various chapters. Like a person who sets a goal to lose weight, you will set a goal in your mind and heart today, and you will begin working hard to lose hurts that have been keeping you from your destiny and the land of promise. Those pounds that you added on by enduring sleepless nights and days of uncertainty, lack of trust, and unstable relationships must go. I declare in Jesus' name that you have a supernatural release from everything or everyone that has bound or hindered you from going forth and being all that God has called you to be.

Readers, let the hurt go! Do not continue to live your life in fear and beneath your God-given privileges. You have a reason and a right to trust God. As you release, ask the Father to fill those areas of hurt with love, joy, and peace. Learn how to set others free with whom you can identify as they carry their hurt baggage around. We can have mercy on others because we know that hurt does not come from a specific person or source; a series of events may cause us to hurt, such as our spouses, children, family members, friends, employers, and even saints. No matter where is the source of the hurt, we must go back to Jesus, who is the heart-fixer. Regardless of what we suffer, God is faithful! We cannot afford to let ourselves stay in this condition any longer; we must forgive, forget, and move forward. I do not mean that you must forget the action, but you must forget the pain associated with the hurt. Let the Father bring you out, and do as the songwriter stated: be better, stronger, and wiser because of what you have endured. If this book helps one person who has been hurt, who was on the verge of throwing in the towel, then my writing will not be in vain.

From Bitter to Better Scriptures

- And the LORD shall make thee the head, and not the tail; and thou shalt be above only, and thou shalt not be beneath (Deuteronomy 28:13).
- I will praise thee; for I am fearfully and wonderfully made: marvellous are thy works; and that my soul knoweth right well (Psalm 139:14).
- No weapon that is formed against thee shall prosper; and every tongue that shall rise against thee in judgment thou shalt condemn. This is the heritage of the servants of the LORD, and their righteousness is of me, saith the LORD (Isaiah 54:17).
- For I reckon that the sufferings of this present time are not worthy to be compared with the glory which shall be revealed in us (Romans 8:18).
- And the peace of God, which passeth all understanding, shall keep your hearts and minds through Christ Jesus (Philippians 4:7).

- But my God shall supply all your need according to his riches in glory by Christ Jesus (Philippians 4:19).
- In every thing give thanks: for this is the will of God in Christ Jesus concerning you (1 Thessalonians 5:18).
- Now unto him that is able to keep you from falling, and to present you faultless before the presence of his glory with exceeding joy. To the only wise God our Saviour, be glory and majesty, dominion and power, both now and ever. Amen (Jude 24-25).

CPSIA information can be obtained at www.ICGtesting.com
Printed in the USA
BVOW030426311012

304252BV00001B/2/P